There is always something going on at the farm! 30 awesome farm illustrations are looking forward to be discovered and colored.

We hope you have lots of fun coloring and doodling :-)

Name of the artist

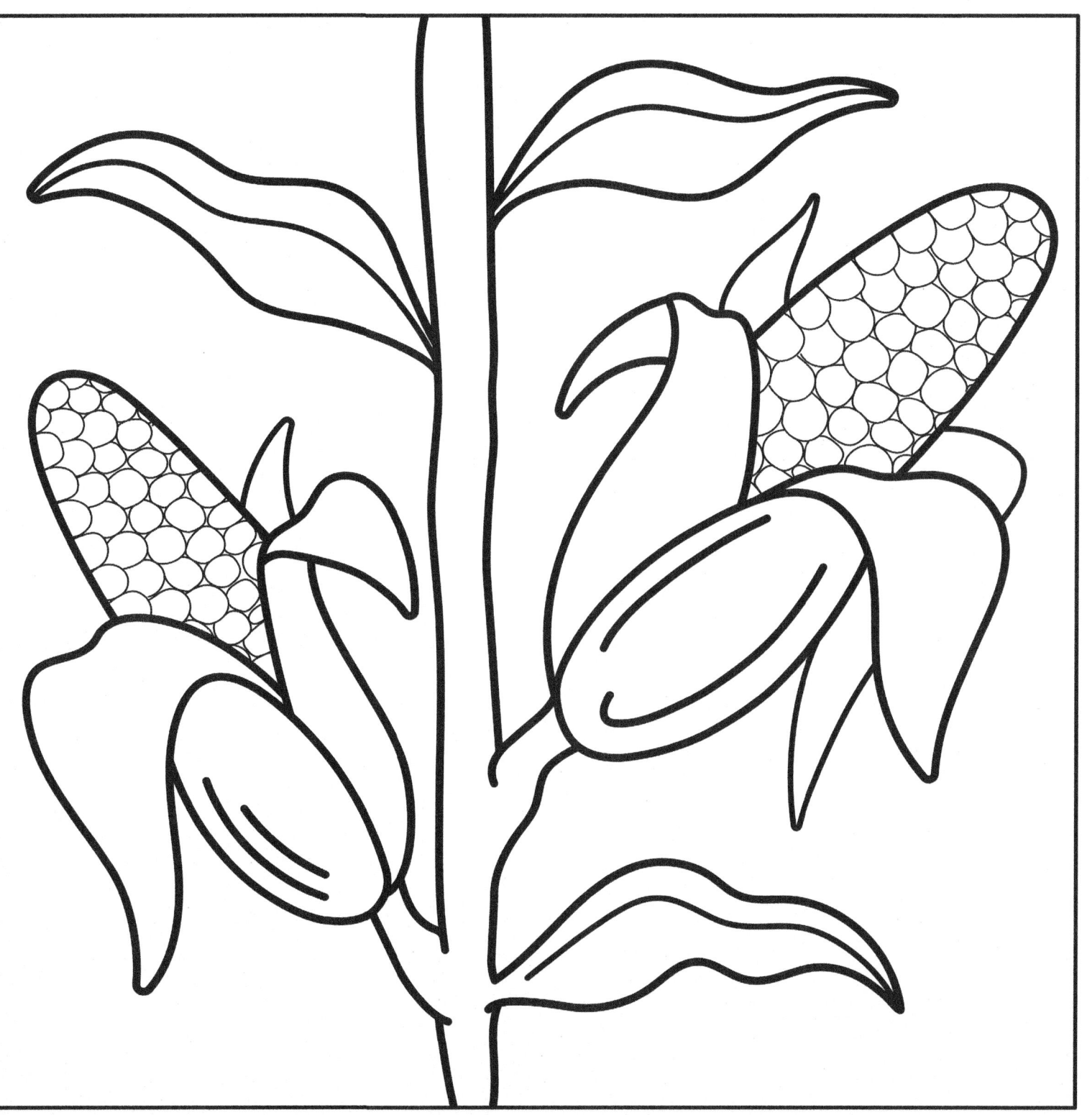

We hope you liked this book! It would mean a lot to us to receive feedback in form of a rating on Amazon or via e-mail at booksbykwabu@gmail.com.

Don't forget to scan the QR-Code below or visit kwabu.com to download your free coloring book!

@booksbykwabu   @booksbykwabu

THANK YOU!
:-)

ISBN: 979-8599415916

© 2021 kwabu - All rights reserved

Imprint:
Jonas Kaiser
Fustenburgstr. 4
50935 Cologne
Germany

Printed in Great Britain
by Amazon